EXTRAORDINARY RENDITIONS

ESSENTIAL POETS SERIES 264

**Canada Council   Conseil des Arts
for the Arts   du Canada**

**ONTARIO ARTS COUNCIL
CONSEIL DES ARTS DE L'ONTARIO**

an Ontario government agency
un organisme du gouvernement de l'Ont

Canadä

Guernica Editions Inc. acknowledges the support of the Canada Council
for the Arts and the Ontario Arts Council. The Ontario Arts Council
is an agency of the Government of Ontario.

We acknowledge the financial support of the Government of Canada.

Niki Lambros

EXTRAORDINARY RENDITIONS

GUERNICA
EDITIONS

TORONTO – BUFFALO – LANCASTER (U.K.)
2019

Anna van Valkenburg, general editor
Elana Wolff, poetry editor
Cover and interior design: Errol F. Richardson
Cover image: *Russian, St Christopher with dog head*
(attributed to Mihail Kirikov, 1910)
Guernica Editions Inc.
1569 Heritage Way, Oakville, (ON), Canada L6M 2Z7
2250 Military Road, Tonawanda, N.Y. 14150-6000 U.S.A.
www.guernicaeditions.com

Distributors:
University of Toronto Press Distribution,
5201 Dufferin Street, Toronto (ON), Canada M3H 5T8
Gazelle Book Services, White Cross Mills
High Town, Lancaster LA1 4XS U.K.

First edition.
Printed in Canada.

Legal Deposit – Third Quarter
Library of Congress Catalog Card Number: 2018967804
Library and Archives Canada Cataloguing in Publication
Title: Extraordinary renditions / Niki Lambros
Names: Lambros, Niki, 1963- author.

Series: Essential poets ; 264.
Description: Series statement: Essential poets series ; 264 | Poems.
Identifiers: Canadiana 20190045442 | ISBN 9781771833868 (softcover)

Classification: LCC PS8623.A48485 E98 2019 | DDC C811/.6—dc23

Contents

            … The old man rose and gazed into my face
and said that was official recognition
that I was now a dual citizen.

He therefore desired me when I got home
to consider myself a representative
and to speak on their behalf in my own tongue.

Their embassies, he said, were everywhere
but operated independently
and no ambassador would ever be relieved.

—from "The Republic of Conscience"
Opened Ground: Selected Poems 1966-1996, by Seamus
Heaney

The Whirlwind

То есть как же это они основали?
да и что значит вообще основать город или государство?
Что ж: они пришли и по кирпичу положили что ли?*

Somewhere in Phoenicia
before recorded time,
Zeus stole Europa,
sister of Cadmus.
She was never seen again.
"Go search the whole world!"
her father said to Cadmus,
"do not return without my daughter."

Cadmus went to Delphi
to hear the oracle:
"Forget that foolish quest,
this is my word:
Follow the sacred cow,
marked with the half-moon.
When she lies down,
exhausted from wandering,
there you shall found your city."
"I will," said Cadmus,
and so he founded Thebes.

But before the sacrifice of the cow
to Selene, goddess of the moon,
he sent his men to a spring
to bring the Ismenian water.
There lay the Hydra.
It woke, and slew them all.
The dragon was the dog
of Ares, god of war;
when he discovered the slaughter
Cadmus killed it with his sword.

Then Athena appeared:
"Take the teeth from its jaws
and sow them in the ground."
Cadmus obeyed.
The soil trembled, the thousand seeds
sprouted into life-in-death,
the naked warriors rose. Fierce, turning,
blood-veiled eyes, fingers talon-poised,
mouths gaping, teeth and growl
were all their weapons.

From his hidden vantage
Cadmus trembled at their numbers.
"How will I control these savages?"
he wondered; then his cunning

calmed him. He palmed a stone
and threw it into their midst,
smashing the skull of one.

As that man was falling,
frenzy seized the rest.
Circling like fighting cocks,
suspicion in every eye,
they tore at one another
ripping blindly at any flesh
all the hours of the day.

By evening, only five were left.
Then Cadmus said to those fragments,
"Come, my men. We must away
to sow the fields of the world."

---

*In what sense did they found it?
And what is meant by founding a city or a state?
Did they go and each lay a brick, do you suppose?
—from **The Brothers Karamazov**

The Brazen Bull

We know from Aristotle's *Rhetoric*,
about an ambitious man called Falarais,
of whom Stesichorus warned,
"Give no allegiance to this man, nor unchecked power;
though he has built you walls
and channelled in free water, these he did
only to seduce; but given place and time,
his sword becomes his scythe.
He's brought his god:
Phoenician Baal has come through Crete to Rhodes,
who is so strong our people call him Zeus,
and Sicilians throughout Argentium worship him,
forgetting their own traditions day by day.
Listen! To thank him for gentrification,
will we reward this foreigner with—*all*?"

They shouted him down quickly enough.
These people wanted the agora expanded,
maybe moved downtown. Coffee houses
to meet in, things that make life convenient
and maximize leisure time. "Anyway, a god
is a god, and if the golden calf brings wealth,
why, now, let him pasture." That's what they said
then. Further, according to Lucian, this:

4

Absolute power. So quickly did this builder
become a subduer, a tearer-down,
snicking off stalk-tops or uprooting outright,
the people were cowed before they could raise their heads.
Nobility was courted; he did enjoy
the tribute, gifts and pomp of office,
but most of all, he liked to show his might
in shows of war. In other words, the usual.

Erasmus also wrote of Falarais,
as did Pindar. The story goes
that when this king's ascendance reached its zenith,
his subjects, free, as it were, from the duty of government,
became a people of entertainments, sports and war.
These occupations had royal approval,
and most forgot the dignity of liberty
(—*so what*. They lived so long ago,
in the 6th century BC.) *Anyhoo*,
here's the important part: an Attic brazier,
Perilaus, bringing a majestic gift
in hopes of winning imperial favour, journeyed
to that calm realm. This sculptor of bronze
was so renowned, Falarais received him readily.
His gift, as one may read in Diodorus,
was this: a huge, bronze bull, with straining
head muscles rippling as though it were live,

the pointed horns atop as sharp as poniards,
curved and rooted in the massive skull.
With nostrils flared and eye-holes filled with carbuncles,
and the mouth open as if bellowing its rage—

let's just say the king was impressed. Perilaus
then began to disclose less obvious splendours:
Under the giant belly held high
by the tree-like limbs, a brazier filled with coals
was set, and on the beast's left side was cut
a door by which a man could be put in
the hollow bull; the fire lit, he'd cook
slowly to death, his flesh sticking to the hot
red metal, searing him like a roast.

This was a lot to take. Falarais imagined
turning the lock (the bull's colossal phallus
held the mechanism) and letting
down the trap to shove the victim in.
"Such ingenuity in torturing,
where did you learn it?" Falarais inquired dryly.
"O King, the best is yet to tell," he answered,
almost beside himself with pride in his own
cleverness. "This magnificent head
is shrewdly fitted from within with flutes
so carved and poised as to transform the screams

of the broiling evil-doer in the gut
to sound as though it lows! The cries of pain
will give you pleasure as they play through the pipes in the
nostrils!"

Falarais stood silently considering this
addition, while Perilaus longed to hear his genius
praised and to receive his kingly reward.
"Tell me," said Falarais, finally,
"where did you find a craftsman
to fit flutes in a brazen bull's head
which would make music of tortured screams?
Surely he knew to what purpose
his cunning service would be put?
And when the smelters saw the cast,
and a hole where better art is seamless,
and when they bolted the hinges on, and fit the lock,
and when they set it on its dais and mounted the brazier,
did no one feel squeamish about his task?
None object, or, if they were not slaves,
revolt against such cruel enterprise?"

Not a bad question. And one to which Perilaus
did not reply because the king had ordered
the trap-door opened, and motioned
him nearer. "Demonstrate for me

the way the pipes operate."
Yes, the door was locked, the coals were lit,
the metal seared, and the head-flutes demonstrated.

But Perilaus didn't die in there. No,
Falarais had him pulled out at the last
minute, and thrown off a cliff. Still unsoiled,
the bull was kept hidden in the palace. But rumour wailed
the secret to the mob, who called it an urban myth.
Artists boldly smashed taboos prohibiting
instruments of torture from being called art.

The media's slick spin made the tyrant
merciful, people even said he was getting soft.
Telemachus heard of it, brought his armies and launched
his liberating forces. During the regime change,
the bull was found, but Telemachus was no wimp.
He put Falarais in there, and listened to that music
in an armchair, while sipping fine wine.
It's hard to imagine those ancient times,
people worshipping calves and all.

The Beating of Lakis

The 3rd century saint Mavrikios
and his son, the martyr Fotios,
appear in the icon to be content.
The father, whipped with a barbed scourge,
bloody, covered in honey and in wasps,
and tied to a tree, head inclined downward
toward the body of his beheaded boy,
yet raises his eyes to heaven.

Today is their Feast Day.
The vicious *bios* read this morning
recalled my questions for these
converts, the repentant killers
from the infamous Theban legion.
Did they even feel the lash,
or was it grace that healed them?
Did they grit their teeth behind their smiles?
The icon will not say
one way or the other. Like flies in amber
the scene is set and no one dares
interpret, least of all myself.

But I remember too, my ancient abbess
on this same day some years before
met her nephew Lakis in the church, the lad

she had not seen in decades, said
to him off-handedly,
"Laki, remember when
your father tied you to a tree
and whipped you all day?"
He smiled, lips compressed and twisted, then
he turned his eyeballs into knives
and cut her throat with them.

The Martyrdom of St Christopher

"… the names of some saints have been deleted from the General
Calendar …"
　　—*motu proprio* of Paul VI for the reform of the Liturgical calendar, 1969

"Tell me his crimes!"
"Sire, he has misled two whole platoons,
they've all gone AWOL!"
"What's that? The dogfaced man
has always been a faithful, cunning cur,
an ugly snout to count on.
What happened to rob him of his growl?"
"Sire, he follows the crucified slave
and calls himself a pacifist.
They follow him, and will not sacrifice
to any of our gods."
"Leave him to our dungeonmasters,
they'll bring him to heel."

The tyrant's prisons burst with men
in chains and used to every
machine of pain and torture.
Only Reprobus—for that was
his name—is kept apart,
to see no human face.

Confined to nakedness
he may not sleep
a quarter hour before a bell's rung
in his ear through days and nights
for weeks on end.
Whenever he has strength,
he paces in his cage.

"Still bloody-minded, is he?
We'll try a different company.
Bring those whores Akylina and Kalliniki,
let them seduce and charm
his monk-like fervour till it shrinks,
and lust restore his potency.
Venus and Mars will turn him
back to his proper gods,
we'll see him fetch again."

(One thousand seven hundred twenty years pass
before a Cardinal, chosen for his sense,
smiles at this folly as he reads. Such men,
he knows, fanatics, never break
until like oaks they are reduced by fire
to humble ash. He takes a glass
of wine with him to bed, continuing

the Life which by his penstroke will be
disappeared from future calendars.)

"What, he will not yield?"
"No, Sire, but now those women
are spinning orisons —"
"Decamp them to the block,
let the axe fall on their necks,
and to the brazen chamber
he will go, to feel a fire below him heat
his knees, burning in its gut! But listen,
when he finds his god cannot deliver
from fiery furnaces, then let him beg
to serve me and recant
his mongrel disposition."

(No, Decius, you've got him all wrong.
He's but a fiction, and such stories always end
the same: he hath a journey, sir, shortly to go.
His master calls him, he must not say no,
et cetera. This dog has let slip secrets
that belong to war, commands anonymous insurgents
of his own, to spy out murderous drones like you.
Ambrose laid 50,000 pagans to his credit,
but none in the last century or two. So,
he must go, and you will be forgotten too.)

The fire was lit, but Christopher, as he was known
among the baptized, hadn't made a sound.
"Has someone put him in there dead? I'll kill the traitor!"
"Sire, he is alive!" "How can that be?"
They open the red-hot box
and out jumps the martyr, praising Iesus.
"Too much offence,"
Decius thinks, I cannot let him live.
"Strike that damned dog head from his shoulders!"

(The Cardinal sighs. Christ.
We've let this legend grow until
it has outstripped the bounds
of decency; are we to believe
in fairy tales? He has lived long:
enough. We'll strike him from the record
lest our faith be lost
by worshipping ideals. From heaven
we'll drag him back to earth
again, back to dust, into oblivion.
We'll teach a better religion.
His medals are revoked.)

What Can Be Said

Trăm năm trong cõi người ta,
Chữ tài chữ mệnh khéo là ghét nhau.
Trải qua một cuộc bể dâu,
Những điều trông thấy mà đau đớn lòng.
Lạ gì bỉ sắc tư phong,
Trời xanh quen thói má hồng đánh ghen.
—Truyện Kiều, Nguyễn Du

Mulberry fields cover the conquered sea.
On some plain genius battles destiny,
Beauty must survive the jealousy
of the Blue Sky.

Earth covers all in time,
striving is all that is not futile,
achieve the purpose despite the absurdity.

When the sea is conquered and covered
in mulberry fields, genius has overtaken
destiny.

The Blue Sky squints
at a maiden's rosy cheeks,
despises and foils them.
But they are heliotropes.

Without the seas between us,
no one would survive.

All I can know I know
is local. Genius lives on
routes, fleeting
ahead, the spirit of the place.

I am considering Viet Nam, brooding on it,
hiding its seeds inside me until they spring up.
I know I have no beauty to fear the sky.
So I will become a mulberry field
and conquer the sea.

The Jungle of Screaming Souls

After Bao Ninh

On the Jungle of Screaming Souls,
helicopters dropped napalm bombs.
The battalion of men beneath
ran in every direction, on fire.
Scattershot blasts, and one by one
machine guns cut them down
until there were only ten.

This happened in 1969
in a diamond-shaped grass clearing,
in the Central Highlands of Vietnam.
The bodies were piled high there,
no jungle ever grew again.

The crows and eagles came,
then the Americans left, rainy season began.
Incinerated animal and human
corpses floated side by side,
bloated, drifted into a stinking marsh.
In time the flood waters receded,
all was dried into thick mud
and rotting blood. From the womb
of the diamond-shaped clearing
the souls of ghosts and devils were born.

There birds cry like humans, they don't
fly. Only there are bamboo shoots
the colour of infected wounds.
Fireflies the size of helmets
shine on the trees and plants
that moan after dark. In '74,
when the recovery team came
to collect the remains, they built
an altar and prayed, secretly.

Incense burns to this day,
but the souls continue screaming.
After that defeat, they refused to depart
to the Other World. Then it was called
the Jungle of Screaming Souls:
the unlucky Battalion 27, lined up
on the diamond-shaped grass.

Dogface

Ο ὥς κυνοπρόσωπος περιγρφόμενος μάρτυς Χριστόφορος
κατήγετο ἐκ χώρα ἀνθρωποφάγων.
One of the race of dogfaced men, the famous martyr Christopher
was from the land of cannibals.

I Hearts and Minds

We were here before our boots hit the ground.
Targets, they are, scheduled for elimination
from the virtual trenches; our weapons make no sound
but bleeps. After the incomplete destruction
we invade in person. The family house,
the little sheep pen behind it—we search them,
find their knives and tools lying in drawers
or on shelves, relics of the unselved.

I thought I was born for this: to sit up, to guard,
to bite. Not like the rest, not at school, not at home.
The doctor had called it by a woman's name,
my syndrome, aristocratic. My nose described
like lingerie, the dark nostrils that stare out like eyes:
retroussé. The ptosis of my jowls, the fibroblasts,
macrotia; I may as well have had the mange.
Dogface, they called me.

Then I joined the pack and soon enough
I was the Alpha, I wanted action. *Man*,
we shot and stomped the hajis, and burned and terrorized,
why not? We had right on our side. To be
all I could be, I found, was to take the life of a dogface,
crushing blood and bone into paste and posing
beside it, asking which is uglier, this death or my face?
That was always good for a laugh. And then one day
I found out who controls the past controls the present,
I have met the enemy, he is not fictional.
He is the ugliness staring back from the mirror
when I look upon it in the dark.
Not a reflection, an emanation, a haunting,
a madness, not Other.

The smashed faces of the greying dead are pictures.
The piled corpses rot and vultures pick them over,
a rural scene. Though I slay him yet will he trust in me,
and death is now their neighbour. No other deliverance
will do. If anyone believes he lives, he must die.
Live as though you're already dead, you may survive.

II The Katharsis of a Dogfight

I used to hate imagination, then I hated memory,
and what could save me from dreams?
Our mission in Falujah was easy: drive the Humvee
through the streets firing not altogether randomly
at military targets. These can be anything that moves,
whatever we say they are. Things have changed
since Geneva. We go to war with the enemy we have.

We do it without irony.
We burn the village to
burn it. The only good civilian
is a dead insurgent.
One night—the one that is known, I mean—
one of the Kill Team
crept from the base and
massacred most of a family,
methodically, not with an
IED. Women and children
only, some with a knife,
and some he set on fire.
He was a sergeant from Tacoma,
now he is unmade,
his head no longer fits
in his helmet, he's quite gone.

I saw myself in his helmet,
one day I tried it on.
It fit my ugly doghead perfectly.

Out amidst the depleted uranium
I learned levity, how to laugh
like Satan. I got all his jokes,
even the ones on me. I shrieked,
aimed into a crowd of dogs
and fired. We tortured them too,
you can see it on YouTube.
Their panicked eyes
just before their heads go "pop!"
it's funny, you see.
My face became fierce,
no longer laughable.
Eventually it could wipe off smiles
as easily as napalm.

The modern dogfight does not involve
two planes. We need no aces or heroes,
no one there to cheer or blame. The drone
is said to act alone, the pilot has no name.
In the small hours outside New Mexico, Afghanistan,
the target is still, a tiny outbuilding,

lone, deserted. It is. It is.
No one is there. Fire the rocket, it's time.
And then, while the targeteer counts back
from seven, the child wanders out.
The shell flies down and bursts
into a puff of light which is flame. The brief
nimbus hangs, collapses in
on itself, the halo disappears
in thick dust, and flesh made dust,
just a bug squash on a screen.
"Was that a kid?" he asks the silence.
"Yeah, I guess it was."
He types it in to me, the booted sentry
on the ground, *Did we just kill a kid?*

I answer: "No, it was a dog. Repeat:
It was a dog." A dog on two legs?
Second Zero was the moment.
A dog? A man? A child? A dog?
Suddenly they're not the same, again.
I've returned to human being
just as it's too late. I see I'm damned,
we're all civilians now. Back,
back from the Rubicon I've stepped,
through the mined field.

Back to base, home base, a run,
a screaming, a dying, a howling.
Inward toward the dead centre
darkness envelops,
'Classified', for no eyes only
my mind's on a loop that plays
again and again, until I was mad
enough to tell. So I was sent to hell.

III Dogface in Quantico

Box, locks,
where are the clocks?
Solo,
sola scriptura,
conscript,
transcript,
cryptic,
crypt,
stripped,
naked
ungripped
warped
weft-bereft
cleft
divided
convicted
convict
racked
trapped
marshalled,
where is the court?
here is the trial

penal
penitent
travesty
injury
suffer me, sir,
the light is always on.

Panopticon,
a camera,
switched on,
a face, a screen,
a presence
invisible
for all the world
unseen.
Overlook
overlord
oversight
Overman
overmanned
unmanned
guarded
barred
charred
card

ward
warden
listen, please
the light is always on.

Signal,
dog-whistle
blown
ears pricked
listening
to silence
to them listening
to him
listening,
still
the light is always on.

Stream of consciousness
scream of a conscientious
abject.
No fall of the dark
day.
Obey
say nothing
no sound

jest
rest
no high zest
say nothing is left
but an old lie,
an unsubstantiated story.

Looking at an Icon
of an Heretical Saint

His hands are stretched above his head,
skin the colour of the dead,
lain upon a tilted table

where the waters had flowed down
into his nose and mouth
over the filthy cloth

as though he were being drowned.
"Tell us where the answer's hidden,
how you planned the armageddon

in the land that once held Eden.
Babylon the great has fallen,
deep into a spider-hole.

There is no hope for you in heaven,
tell us now, tell us now, tell us
again, how, and where, and when."

He did not think he was a martyr,
then. Yea, he did not die, not once,
not one hundred and eighty three times.

Mohammed, why hast thou,
why hast thou forsaken
all around you who were taken?

There was nothing more to say;
it was extracted anyway.
"I knew a man, I knew another,"

he babbled on and on, "oh yes,
she was my brother. It was I
who struck that face, saying, 'prophesy'.

With my terrible sword of vengeance, I
plundered the pearl of great price,"
(and this was later proven true:

The hagiographers had scanned
the bulging vein in his blessed right hand
and said, "Yes, it was surely you.")

It was all done by him from A to Z,
everything since 1993,
including the bombing in Bali,

and shooting John Paul II —
or at least, plotting to.
His little children, 6 and 8,

were locked behind a metal gate
and testified, and testified
until they named everyone they knew.

So now the truth is known.
The icon looks like all the rest,
just a man, tortured to near-death:

ecce homo? The icon's model lies,
unseen, in Guantanamo.

Northern Iraq, 1973

I Archaeology

It was night. The Takbir rose up with the sun.
Allahu Akbar. Allahu Akbar. Allahu Akbar.

II

Heat waved from the burning sand, blurring
the temple and labyrinth walls of the dig.
From the stillness emerged turbaned workers,
flocks of goats, sheep, and camels
driven along to the sound of pickaxes.
Pickaxes, picking at the hard, burnt soil,
excavating, revealing the ancient map
of streets and lanes, foundations, caches.
A surefooted boy ran the maze of dirt paths,
halted before the quarry. *"They've found
something."*—"Where?"—*"At the base of the mound."*
Slowly, the old man rose from his crouch,
following the kicked up dust in the path
to approach the mound. A guard stood by
the Jesuit archaeologist in charge,
acknowledged his right to see, to take.
He knelt beside the small cave,
his eye caught a glint in the sand.
A Christian medal, he turned it in his hand.
"Different period."
Into his pocket. When he peered in
the cave's mouth, cool wind blew out.

A cold gust came out from the small cave.
He put his hand into the darkness and felt it
immediately. He pulled it into the light,
broke the exterior clod of mud in two
exposing the face hidden for centuries.
Babylonian? Assyrian. He'd seen
that head before. He'd seen its body, its wings.

III

His heart, again. He staggered
toward the crowd below the dig site,
through the groupings of men amid the dust
and tunnels, shuffled toward the
scape of domes, minarets, the mosque in black
shadow backed by the disc of the sun.
Dazed and trembling, he arrived
at a tea house. The arak
jittered in his loose grip, he knocked it
back, forced digitalis under his tongue
and waited the necessary seconds.
The graceful tea boy bowed and served.
Sheep doddered by and camels sloped by,
goat bells and glasses jangled softly.
A man led a blind man with a cane.
A madman glowered under his skullcap.
The Jesuit watched, backed by a throng
of various Arabs, sand-covered men,
sounds of the market place surrounded him
twisting his way through the alleys.
He passed the open-hearth furnace
where three men were mongering iron,

hammering one after one on the anvil,
the trinity broken when one stopped and
stared out at him, wiping his burning brow.
One of his eyes was whited-over,
blank, unseeing as an idol's.

IV

Back at the museum, he breathed
to the steady tick of the Arabic clock, its
face telling one in their symbols. The rooms
were filled with catalogued stones, shards,
pedestaled busts and torsos.
He sat at his desk, entered the new finds.
Cleaned, the medallion showed Saint Joseph.
That, he's seen; not much interest there.
Then, the little black stone demon head.
"Evil against evil, Father,"
his Iraqi colleague piped. Suddenly
he noticed it: the clock's pendulum
stopped mid-swing. He lurched
to his desk and collapsed.

V

He had to make certain.
Leaving the building he stumbled
back into the road, past rows of men
prostrate in prayer, the *raka'at*,
up through the canvassed passage lined
with market stalls, women in niqabs.
A furious coach appeared from an archway,
high wheels missed him by inches, the team
of black horses whinnying madly,
long reins held by a black chadored crone,
cackling, eyes crazed. She passed him,
he clutched at his heart through his shirt.

VI

Back on the dig at last, guards with rifles rushed out
aiming, slowed, recognized, and withdrew.
Breathing hard, heaving, he turned into the wind
toward the sun, and saw it.
A shot rang out. Dogs whined
in the distance, growled and snapped.
They stood opposed, elevated each on his hill:
the American priest and the demon *Pazuzu*,
its left arm raised, fist facing out,
its black wings spread.

VII Apocalypse

Did you recognize it?
The last six parts of this poem?
Max von Sydow as the priest?
The dig site was Hatra,
where the story of *The Exorcist* began:
A demon took possession
of a girl in Washington D.C.
Don't you remember that movie?

Hatra is now a desolation,
statues smashed by sledgehammers,
bas relief riddled by machine gun bullets,
temples levelled with explosives.
ISIS took possession
and cleansed the abomination. .

The unwanted gods have all been erased
from Palmyra to Nineveh,
like the Buddhas of Bamiyan,
the first victims, back before it all began
in Afghanistan, March 2001,
smashed, shot up, annihilated by the Taliban.
Remember that? It's like ancient history now,
who can possess it again?

What Happened at Camp X-ray

What happened at Camp X-ray
to make it radioactive?
It became a place to manufacture
facts derived from torture.
In short, GTMO. We claimed
we didn't know what went on.
But we suspected that we knew,
even knew that we knew.
We'd seen it all before and we knew.
What they said was that valuable intelligence—
"Excuse me, what was that, sir?"
Valuable intelligence from 9/11 suspects
was gathered, harvested, from a secret
machine made of both kinds
of people. A reducing factory.

Now, we know what happened
at Camp X-ray, and at other
Camp X-rays. What we can't measure
is the half-life.

The Torture Report

Our intentions were good.
We were developing techniques
to keep our people sane
if they had been captured and tortured.
If some of the enemy suffered,
they'd have done worse to our own
had the tables been turned.
You know they are savages.
They would stop at nothing
to kill us all. Well, that's true.
Fanatics know no boundaries.
They are capable of anything.
They might have stripped our boys down,
splayed and chained them to a concrete floor
and raped them over and over,
or let dogs rape them over and over.
They might have caged them,
naked, in darkness for weeks,
or in blinding light, deprived of sleep,
and raped them with hoses.
They might have captured the innocent
and beaten them bloody, every day,
and left them to freeze that way,
cowering until they stiffened in death.
They might have built prisons

all over the world, secret places
to carry out the obscenities,
run by the children they'd told
to pull the wings off men.
"Forced dependency," they might have said
when asked to explain
the purpose of inflicting this
humiliating, sadistic pain. But that's
insane; and it was us, not them.

Let Everyone Know

"What happened to us in Diwana
was because we were Shia Iraqis,
not Islamists, not Muslim brothers.

"The men from ISIS divided us
into groups, some to be tortured,
some to die by firing squad.
I was fourth in line.
It began, one shot, two shots,
then, to my right, and blood splashed my face,
I saw my daughter in my mind
saying 'father, father.'
The bullet clears my ear, I fall
face down into the trench, still.
One of the killers began to walk by
a man breathing still.
'Leave him to suffer. Let him bleed.'
I felt a great will to live."

Four hours later when it was dark,
Kadhim edged to the Tigris. On the bank
hidden by reeds, he met an injured man.
He too had been shot and put to bleed
into the river. But Abbas could not
live. Kadhim stayed three days,

eating insects and plants.
When Kadhim said he must escape,
Abbas implored him to come back,
and if he could not, to tell.
"Let everyone know
what happened to us in Diwana,
the three days of hell."

The Peloponnesian Wars

Thucydides, an Athenian,
recorded his war believing
its import would surpass all wars.
He thought it would alter
humanity forever.
Two and a half millennia later,
it all happened again,
just as he'd written it.

As with the Athenians,
mistakes were made
that lost the spoils taken,
left the land barren,
and the sons of the people forsaken
rose from the fields of the world,
to claim and reclaim
what couldn't be held. Like sand
that slips through the fingers
of an overplayed hand,
or through an hourglass
that shows time run out,
wasted, a wasteland,
a no-man's land.

The men of ISIS fight,
they seem invincible now.
Their weapons are the best
the world has ever seen, the ones
that were left to the tune
of billions in warehouses
for the taking. Boys
and even girls follow the
song across the seas
to find the desert and die,
their parents asking why
and hearing the empty wind.
The sound of jihad
in their ears, the imam's wail,
the uncomprehending
soldiers line up and fire,
the hail of bullets,
the sheer number of them,
means they win today,
tomorrow. They won't run out,
they've got the oil this whole
fucking war was all about.

There's always someone
to sell them whatever they need,
more ammunition, more bullets,
more tanks, more anti-aircraft weapons,
more rockets, more explosives for IEDs.
But most important to everyone
on their makeshift battlefields
wherever there's a place to bleed
comes the never ending supply of guns.
M249 light machine guns,
MK19 and MK19 MOD 3 grenade machine guns,
M249 machine guns
50 caliber machine guns
M2 machine guns
M60D machine guns
M240B machine guns and rifles,
M14 rifles
CAR-15 automatic rifles
M4 carbines
M16A2 semiautomatic rifles
M107 sniper rifles
SR-XM1110 sniper rifles.
Helicopters, grenade launchers,
they've got them all.
They ride in Humvees,

using the Internet
to post their videos
of journalists and those
they've captured,
beheaded.

It spreads, metastasizes,
from Afghanistan to Iraq
to Syria to Nigeria
and if history is any judge,
goddamn certain
it will find its way back.
Can we ever run
that one last Marathon
to bring even a decade of peace?
Not according to Thucydides.

Boko Haram

We drive through the jungle
we drive across the bush
we drive across the bushland
the bush land the bush land
the jungle we drive through
jump out of the trucks
jump out of the trucks
in a village a village
machine guns machine guns machine guns machine guns
machetes machine guns machine guns
machetes machine guns
machetes machetes machine guns machine guns

Jump out of the trucks
burn all the huts
burn up the huts
scatter the people the people
into the bushland the jungle
corner the schoolhouse the schoolhouse

Western education is a sin against sin against
Western education Western education
a sin is a sin is a sin is a sin is a
this is a *caliphate!*
this is a *caliphate!*

we don't need preaching
we have no preaching
we're gonna teach them
BAYonet BAYonet BAYonet BAYonet
up between her legs
ripping up the wo
man
the wo
man
she can't resist us
who can't resist us
the girls
the girls
two hundred little school girls
another hundred school girls
another hundred school girls
take it till they learn it learn it
STICK STICK STICK STICK
THIS PRICK AND *THIS* PRICK AND *THIS*
PRICK AND *THIS* PRICK AND
THIS PRICK AND *HIS* PRICK AND
take it take it take it take it

The echoing screams
echoing echoing
scream into the jungle
I don't even hear you
nobody can hear you
nobody will hear you
no one is coming
no one is coming

Goodluck Jonathan
didn't do nothing
didn't do nothing
lying through his teeth
lying lying lying lying
even though the headlines
are screaming for attention:
Bring back our girls!
Bring back our girls!
Bring back our girls!
Bring back our girls!

Now Michelle Obama
is holding a placard:
Bring Back Our Girls!
Malala

Malala
is holding a placard
Bring Back Our Girls!
a thousand famous faces
are holding up a placard
and everywhere everywhere
all the common people
are tweeting and *tweeting*
#Bring Back Our Girls!
#Bring Back Our Girls!

Six months go by
and one year goes by and
two years go by and
some, only seven,
of the girls have escaped,
and they're telling the world
what happened what happened
to end their young girlhood
to end their young girlhood
in a tent in a tent
or under the branches
tied with ropes
tied with tied with tied with
more girls are taken

more girls are taken
sold into slavery
slavery slavery.
Twelve year old girls
nine year old girls

Black milk of daybreak
drink it drink it drink it drink it

The Museum of Torture

Not every city has one, of course.
Most people get their fixes
by walking into churches: the *secondary relics*,
jags of metal which splintered bones,
flayed skin from muscle, a bit of Catherine's wheel,
the crucifixion nails, the knouts, barbed whips and flails—
These one dismisses
as spurious, counterfeit, specious shams,
their witness incredible, their day done,
their power to heal the sick long forgotten.

Not so with those *objects de virtu*
displayed in the museum's glass cases:
these are made new, ever-expanding exhibits,
sources of cool-tempered fascination.
Some are crude, like old racks with ropes restored
as if ready.
Some from the time of the Inquisition
lend their names to heavy metal bands:
Iron Maiden, Head Crusher, The Brank,
and Pear of Anguish. This last I have seen:
the dozens of extant exemplars,
crafted with filigree
like Fabergé eggs. Four slender spoons
come together like fitted petals

to shape the metalwork fruit,
fastened on a ridged pin
which opens like a bloom.
Force the bulb into the mouth,
turn the handle on top, the quatro-winged lever
spreads inexorably out, and out,
teeth cracking, shattering
the jaw
in
the mouth
breaking
cranking open
open, lips rip;
thick, sticky streams dribble down the chin.
Before the skull splits, the tongue swells
in the back of the throat, the windpipe blocked,
hypoxia sets in. The heart stops,
it is finished.

So it's worth a trip to the museum of torture,
if only to remember
these have no power
to heal, either.

In My Rooms Which Are like Cells

A wooden cross hangs
by its simple black cord
across the top of a large wooden icon.
The icon shows the virgin-
martyr Paraskevi
holding up an icon
of the dead face of Christ.
This icon is special, it was given to a nun
on the day her hair was cut
and her old name disappeared.
The cross has been hanging atop the icon
for the last fifteen years.

A prayer rope hangs
in a similar triangle
from the corners
of the photo of an ex-lover.
The man's face is bearded, his hair
is long. It also has been on the wall
for over a decade.
Cord, rope, knots, icons
hang in my rooms where I may stare
at them each day, remembering
what they once meant,
marvelling to see them still there.

Acknowledgements

I would like to thank my MA Supervisor Mary di Michele of Concordia University for her unsentimental critical eye, which honed the poems like a laser-beam while still managing to encourage my own style and voice. To my editor at Guernica Editions, Elana Wolff, I owe a debt of gratitude for being such a generous reader of this debut volume, likewise to co-director and president Connie McParland and publisher and editor-in-chief Michael Mirolla, for giving me this start. I'd also like to thank my old friend and advisor from Cambridge, Dr. Malcolm Guite, whose academic and literary support over the years has helped me to become a confident poet. Without my colleague and constant reader Will Vallieres I'd surely have lost that confidence. And as always, I thank my parents Dean and Dorathea Lambros for their unfailing and diverse contributions to this and all my work.

About the Author

Niki Lambros was born in New York, NY, immigrated to Canada after the 9/11 attacks and became a citizen in 2011. She holds a BA in English Literature from Bard College, an MA in Theology, and an MA in Creative Writing from Concordia University, where she is presently working on a PhD in Poetry and Translation. After expatriating to Greece in 1987, she became a Greek Orthodox monastic residing in Greece, Jerusalem, and South Korea, resigning the order in 2000. She relinquished US citizenship in 2014 and lives in Montreal.

Printed in July 2019
by Gauvin Press,
Gatineau, Québec